WISDOM THROUGHOUT THE AGES

WISDOM THROUGHOUT THE AGES

HERMAN GUY

AuthorHouse™
1663 Liberty Drive
Bloomington, IN 47403
www.authorhouse.com
Phone: 1-800-839-8640

© 2012 by Herman Guy. All rights reserved.

No part of this book may be reproduced, stored in a retrieval system, or transmitted by any means without the written permission of the author.

Published by AuthorHouse   04/25/2012

ISBN: 978-1-4685-4770-2 (sc)
ISBN: 978-1-4685-4769-6 (e)

Library of Congress Control Number: 2012901578

Any people depicted in stock imagery provided by Thinkstock are models, and such images are being used for illustrative purposes only.
Certain stock imagery © Thinkstock.

This book is printed on acid-free paper.

Because of the dynamic nature of the Internet, any web addresses or links contained in this book may have changed since publication and may no longer be valid. The views expressed in this work are solely those of the author and do not necessarily reflect the views of the publisher, and the publisher hereby disclaims any responsibility for them.

CONTENTS

Lesson/Warm Up Activity/Guest Entertainment xiii
Action.. 1
Adaptability & Opportunity 2
Adversity & Challenges 3
Advice 5
Aging... 6
Alcohol 7
Anger & Patience 8
Animals & Babies 11
Business & Career.................................. 12
Choice & Common Sense........................ 15
Combat & War 16
Complaining & Criticism 23
Conceit.. 24
Conscience.. 25
Control 27
Courage 28
Defeat & Determination 30
Direction & Encouragement 32
Diplomacy 33
Discipline... 34

- Dreams 36
- Education 38
- Enthusiasm & Excellence 41
- Envy & Forgiveness 42
- Experience & Facts 43
- Flattery & Speaking 44
- Freedom & Patriotism 45
- Friends & Family 47
- Generosity & Humor 51
- Goals & Success 52
- Gossip 59
- Happiness & Heart 60
- Home & Hope 61
- Honor 62
- Humility 67
- Integrity 68
- Kindness 69
- Labor & Laziness 70
- Law 71
- Leadership 72
- Lies & Truth 75
- Life & Death 76
- Listening 92
- Love 93
- Loyalty & Marriage 100
- Miscellaneous 102
- Neighbors 106
- Opinions 107

Parenting & Children 109
Pessimism/Optimism 111
Preparation... 112
Pride 113
Promises & Responsibility 114
Reputation.. 115
Silence.. 118
Sincerity 120
Smiling 121
Spirituality.. 123
Tact 128
Teamwork... 129
Time 130
Trouble.. 132
Trust 133
Understanding... 134
Wisdom... 135
Words.. 136
Youth... 137

As a Historian, I've had the opportunity to study various cultures and their religious views, spiritual beliefs, and philosophical thoughts throughout the ages. While doing so, I came across many quotes, proverbs, and popular phrases. Some of these were very familiar, while others were obscure and/or variations of some more common sayings. I began collecting the ones that appeared to be anonymous, and even added a few of my own creation. I started utilizing this compilation for classroom review, student warm-up activities, and even as a means to entertain guests at my home. They help foster discussion, debate, and higher level thinking skills. Many of them are also motivating and inspirational. What I now share with you, took over fifteen years to collect and publish. I truly hope you find this collection as interesting, entertaining, and useful as I do. Best wishes through your life's journeys. Enjoy and have fun . . .

This book is dedicated to my wonderful wife, Abbie Capobianco, and to our beautiful baby boy, Mason Alexander Guy.

LESSON/WARM UP ACTIVITY/GUEST ENTERTAINMENT

1) Post the quote (and following questions) on the board, overhead projector, or piece of paper.
2) What do YOU believe this quote to mean?
3) Is the quote literal or interpretive?
4) Do you agree or disagree with the quote? WHY?
5) Student or Guests have 2 minutes (timed) to work on the questions individually or as a team.
6) Call on students/guests to share their responses (1 minute time limit).
7) Eventually, pick half of the class/guests to agree with the quote, and the other half to disagree. Repeat steps 2-6. They then stand up and debate (conduct a point/counter-point).

ACTION

- The thing to try, when all else fails, is to try again
- Giving something another try is better than an alibi.
- Other people may see your deeds, but God sees your motives.
- He who asks a question may be a fool for five minutes; he who never asks a question remains a fool forever.
- Asking saves a lot of guesswork.
- Those who wish to move mountains must start by carrying away small stones.
- It is often easy identifying a problem, but another matter in taking action to correct it.
- Once you believe, you can achieve.
- If it can be imagined, it can be accomplished.

ADAPTABILITY & OPPORTUNITY

- Most people are willing to adapt, not because they see the light, but because they feel the heat.
- The world changes so fast, that you couldn't stay wrong all the time if you tried.
- The trouble with opportunity is that it's always more recognizable going than coming.
- Opportunity may knock, but it never turns the knob and walks in.
- He who kills time buries opportunities.
- Luck is what happens when preparation meets opportunity.
- When opportunity knocks, the pessimist complains about the noise.
- Ability, without opportunity, may lead to nowhere.

ADVERSITY & CHALLENGES

- He who wants a place in the sun should expect blisters.
- It takes both rain and sunshine to make a rainbow.
- Sometimes you find you're up against it, because you back up instead of going ahead.
- Prosperity makes friends, while adversity tries them.
- Adversity causes some men to break, and others to break records.
- He who has not met adversity knows not his own strength.
- Heaven prepares good men with crosses.
- The best way to solve your problem is to help someone else solve theirs.
- If a care is too small to be turned into a prayer, it is too small to be made into a burden.
- Knowledge is power.
- Time heals all wounds.
- Everything in life is what you make of it.

- Prosperity would not be so welcome, without the taste of adversity.
- Springtime would not be so pleasant, without the winter that preceded it.
- Laughing is inexpensive medicine.

ADVICE

- Guidance means that I can count on God; commitment means that God can count on me.
- Advising a fool is like beating the air with a stick.
- The way to be successful is to follow the advice that you give others.
- Advice is one thing most people would rather give than get.
- A pint of example is worth a gallon of advice.
- Do not waste time with the negative pessimist; it is better spent on someone who is aware enough to respond with a positive attitude.
- Good judgment often comes from experience, and experience usually comes from bad judgment.

AGING

- When you were born, you cried and the world rejoiced. Live your life in such a way that when you die, the world will cry and you will rejoice.
- He whose night out, is followed by a day in, is growing old.
- One cannot help being old, but one can resist being aged.
- There's many a good tune in an old fiddle.
- Age, in number of years and the ability to procreate, does not determine adulthood; complete self-reliance does.
- If the music seems too loud, then you're probably too old.
- The memory of who we were and what we did, will impact and continue in the lives of others.

ALCOHOL

- Liquor doesn't wash away troubles; it only irrigates them a little.
- Drinking men commit suicide on installment plans.
- Only weak characters lean on strong drinks.
- Boozers are losers.
- Those who say things drive them to drink should walk.
- There is nothing wrong with drinking like a fish, provided you drink what a fish drinks.
- No alcoholic is really anonymous.
- It is one thing to consume a vice, another to be consumed by a vice.

ANGER & PATIENCE

- Anger is just one letter short of danger.
- Hot words never resulted in cool judgment.
- He who has a sharp tongue soon cuts his own throat.
- The greatest remedy for anger is delay.
- When a man is wrong and won't admit it, he always becomes angry.
- If you speak when you're angry, you'll make the best speech you'll ever regret.
- Anger makes your mouth work faster than your mind.
- Every time you give someone a piece of your mind, you make your head a little emptier.
- Anger is a wind that blows out the lamp of the mind.
- Fighting for what is right often turns into fighting for what is left.
- Those who fly into a rage usually make a bad landing.

- The best time to keep your shirt on is when you're hot under the collar.
- Those who lose their temper should not look for it.
- Nothing will cook your goose faster than a boiling-hot temper.
- Those who lose their temper usually lose.
- To stay out of hot water, keep a cool head.
- Poise is the act of raising your eyebrows instead of raising the roof.
- You can't get rid of your temper by losing it.
- The world needs more warm hearts, and fewer hotheads.
- You are not dynamic simply because you blow your top.
- Today's temper tantrum is tomorrow's antiestablishment demonstration.
- When someone loses their temper, their reason goes on vacation.
- Hitting the ceiling is the wrong way to move up in the world.
- Anger is an enemy within which you must kill, but beware for it is a dangerous prey.

- Anyone can follow the path of fear to the gate of anger, and find it an easy march to the house called hatred.
- Anger resides in the laps of fools.
- Temper is what gets most of us into trouble; pride is what keeps us there.
- Patience, in one moment of anger, will save you a hundred days of sorrow.
- Patience is the ability to count down before blasting off.
- You cannot sow, and then reap, on the same day.
- Patience is a virtue that carries a lot of weight.

ANIMALS & BABIES

- Possibly the reason why a dog is such a good friend is that his tail wags and not his tongue.
- The reason a dog is man's best friend is because he does not pretend; he proves it.
- You can lead a horse to water, but you can't make it drink.
- If you growl all day, it's natural to feel dog-tired at night.
- Babies are angels whose wings grow shorter as their legs grow longer.
- Babies are little rivets in the bonds of marriage.

BUSINESS & CAREER

- Actions speak louder than words.
- The harder you work towards your goals, the luckier you get.
- There is an island of opportunity in the middle of every difficulty.
- Always seize the day.
- The race towards quality has no finish line.
- You become successful the moment you begin working towards a worthwhile goal.
- Teamwork divides the task and doubles the success.
- The only thing needed to be a winner, is to give all that you have.
- Success is a journey, never a destination.
- Find ways of making things happen, not waiting for them to happen.
- You can only fail if you stop too soon.
- If you believe you can, or if you believe you can't, you're right on both counts.

- The way to accelerate your success is to double your failure rate.
- An ounce of action is worth more than an ocean of intention.
- Never let the shadow of failure block the sunlight of success.
- Don't do enough to get by; do enough to get ahead.
- Sometimes, the desire to succeed and the willingness to learn are more important than age or experience.
- An obstacle is merely an opportunity that is unrecognized.
- Professional success is worthless without personal and family success.
- Feed opportunities and starve problems.
- Planning should be your servant, never your master.
- Success is sometimes going from one failure to another, without losing enthusiasm.
- Excellence is not an act, but a habit.
- Try not to be a person of success, but rather a person of virtue and then success shall come.
- Organization is the key to success.
- To question yourself is useful; to doubt yourself is not.

- You can only fail by not allowing yourself to succeed.
- Better to have tried and failed, than to never have tried at all.
- When you refuse to accept anything but the best, you will often receive it.
- Whatever is worth doing is worth doing well.
- The struggle to improve is a never ending process.
- The early bird catches the worm.
- There are no problems; only opportunities to be creative.
- Any organization is only as strong as its weakest link.
- Don't trip over dollars to obtain pennies.

CHOICE & COMMON SENSE

- Be careful which road you choose, for you may end up on it for many miles.
- No one learns to make right decisions without being free to make wrong ones.
- Choice, not change, determines human destiny.
- One should give a lot of thought to a sudden decision.
- To every man is given the power of choice.
- Common sense is not always so common.
- Emotion makes the world go round, but common sense keeps it from going too fast.
- You initially make your choices, but eventually your choices make you.

COMBAT & WAR

- Never be taken by surprise.
- In the heat of battle, always remain cool.
- A true warrior, in the menacing presence of danger or death, retains his self-possession.
- In the midst of catastrophes, keep level headed.
- Combat is not solely a matter of brute force; it is also an intellectual engagement.
- Keep your friends close, and your enemies closer.
- We should own as enemies in war, only those who prove worthy of being friends in peace.
- The word of a true warrior should be a sufficient guarantee for the truthfulness of an assertion.
- A warrior refuses to compromise his character by slight humiliation.
- For a true warrior to hasten death or to court it is akin to cowardice.
- Do not bare the sword in vain.

- Those who live by the sword will most surely die by the sword.
- The best won victory is the one obtained without the shedding of blood.
- The ultimate ideal of an honorable warrior is peace.
- True destruction comes from the inside out.
- A man who has nothing to lose is a dangerous foe.
- Never let your opponent see all of your skills.
- The sword is always conquered by the mind.
- Never reduce the enemy to a faceless evil; always understand the forces that shaped them.
- Be aware of your environment, but never let it affect you in ways you don't desire.
- Only the gallant can find a way to win in the face of certain defeat.
- Even the sharpest blade grows dull over time.
- Expect the unexpected, and anticipate the inconceivable.
- When reason fails, force prevails.

- Victory does not always come to the most powerful; but to those whose heart will not accept defeat.
- He who has hope can never be conquered.
- Loyalty to an ideal, may blind you to the true enemy.
- It is not the size of the man in the fight that counts, but rather the size of the fight in the man.
- Fear and terror may accomplish what reason and understanding cannot.
- A life is a small price to pay, if it ensures a better world for those who come later.
- A coward dies a thousand deaths; a hero dies but once.
- A true hero is not measured by the size of his strength, but by the size of his heart.
- A good commander takes advantage of chance, but not if it means abandoning a long term strategy for short term gains.
- Borrowing strength may build weakness.
- An attack without reason is cowardly indeed.
- Death is a natural result of war.

- Once it's too late for talk, you have to commit to fight.
- When facing overwhelming odds in battle, you must change the equation.
- A powerful foe's resources should be diminished before confrontation.
- There are more ways to defeat a foe than a direct assault.
- The warrior who picks his battlefield has the advantage.
- From defeat, ultimate victory may emerge.
- A slow thrust makes no sound to warn the enemy, but a wild slash sings a warning to even the blindest of foes.
- Victory comes to those that believe in it the most.
- The strongest chain is defined by its weakest link.
- Without occasional skirmishes, your forces may grow weak.
- Complacency enables the opposition to strengthen, unseen, in the shadows.
- Never focus on a short term goal, at the expense of a long term gain.
- Combat is won by a series of decisive moves.

- Sometimes, those who are most honorable are also most deadly.
- Define the ground, and you command the battle.
- Trust no ice until tread upon; no shield until tested; and no sword until hacking . . . or risk being bested.
- The flaw of power is arrogance.
- Villains may come and go, but evil never dies.
- There can be no true victory, without honor.
- The most effective weapon against your enemy is the one that remains unknown to them.
- Study your opponent, and defeat them before the fight begins.
- Desperate times may call for desperate measures.
- The most dangerous enemy is the one with nothing to lose.
- When you commit your total awareness to only one opponent, you open yourself to attack from others.
- Play the game like a pawn, and you will be sacrificed like one.
- Always be aware of the strike you don't expect.

- A great strategist takes advantage of every opportunity.
- A true warrior may suffer the bitter taste of defeat, but never will he stomach the shame of surrender.
- Victory is not won by the power you wield; it is determined by the skill in which you wield it.
- If you plan to win, and prepare to win, then you can expect to win.
- The first lesson in hunting your prey, is knowing your prey.
- There is no victory without some sacrifice.
- Growth is the sole purpose of evil.
- Heroes are made, not born.
- Sometimes, you can't fight new threats with old rules.
- Overconfidence and ignorance are always a deadly combination.
- Flying blind is a poor strategy.
- The best warriors can turn an opponent's apparent advantages against them.
- Force brings a certain measure of security, but true power can only be derived from knowledge.
- There is more to war than killing.

- Without knowing your enemy, a hundred victories may still result in defeat.
- If you begin to take the battlefield, then take the battlefield.
- Never mistake kindness for weakness.
- Just because someone won't fight, doesn't mean they can't fight.
- Might makes right.
- Liberty has never been won, except by deeds of war.
- A true warrior is a fighting philosopher.
- Little guppies shouldn't swim with the sharks.
- If you're unwilling to bite, then don't bark.
- If a conflict is serious enough for war, then commit yourself to total war and total victory.
- All war comes with a high price.
- Any fight worth fighting is worth winning.
- In times of peace, prepare for war.

COMPLAINING & CRITICISM

- Sweep the snow from your own front door before you complain about the frost on your neighbor's tiles.
- He who forgets the language of gratitude can never be on speaking terms with happiness.
- He who constantly criticizes his inferiors hasn't any.
- You'll never move up if you are continually running somebody down.
- He who blows out the other fellow's candle won't make his own shine any brighter.
- If you're not big enough to stand criticism, you're too small to be praised.
- He who throws dirt loses ground.
- Negative people enjoy wallowing in negativity.

CONCEIT

- He who sings his own praises seldom gets the right pitch.
- Those who are conceited have swelling heads and shrinking brains.
- He who is full of himself is likely to be quite empty.
- He who falls in love with himself will have no rivals.
- An egotist's only good feature is that he seldom gossips about other people.
- Conceit is the only disease that makes everyone sick but the one who has it.

CONSCIENCE

- Conscience is something that feels terrible when everything else feels wonderful.
- Conscience doesn't keep you from doing anything; it just keeps you from enjoying it.
- When a man won't listen to his conscience, it's usually because he doesn't want advice from a stranger.
- Many people have their bad memory to thank for their clear conscience.
- Conscience is a playback of the small voice that told you not to do it in the first place.
- Conscience is that inner voice that warns us someone is watching.
- The line is often busy when conscience wishes to speak.
- He who has a fight with his conscience and loses, actually wins.
- A conscience is what makes you feel guilty for doing what it wasn't strong enough to keep you from doing.

- The world would be better off if people paid as much attention to their consciences as they do to their neighbor's opinions.
- Conscience, like a pencil, needs to be sharpened occasionally.
- The testimony of a good conscience is worth more than a dozen character witnesses.
- Conscience is that small voice that yells so loud the morning after.
- There is no better tranquilizer than a clear conscience.
- Sitting alone with one's conscience, may be judgment enough for some.

CONTROL

- To stay out of hot water, keep a cool head.
- Control your thoughts, for they may break into words at any time.
- He who talks without thinking runs more risks than he who thinks without talking.
- He who thinks twice before saying nothing is wise.
- He who lives without self-control is exposed to grievous ruin.
- Poise is the act of raising your eyebrows instead of the roof.
- He that would govern others first should be master of himself.
- Character does not reach its best until it is controlled, harnessed, and disciplined.

COURAGE

- Do what you fear, and the death of fear is certain.
- Courage is not how you fall, but how you get back up.
- An inferior man blames others, a superior man holds himself accountable.
- A true champion has tried, failed, and fallen numerous times, but has never quit.
- When you know something to be wrong, you must find the courage to correct it.
- Conscience is the root of true courage.
- Courage is being scared to death and climbing back in the saddle again.
- Courage is doing right, even when everyone around you is doing wrong.
- Courage is unworthy, unless exercised in the cause of righteousness.
- Tranquility is courage in repose.
- Truly brave men are ever serene.

- Courage is what it takes to stand up and speak; courage is also what it takes to sit down and listen.
- Courage is the power to let go of the familiar.
- He who lacks courage thinks with his legs.
- Courage is fear that has said its prayers.
- He who does not dare will not get his share.
- When there is no money, half is gone; when there is no courage, all is gone.
- To the brave and true, nothing is difficult.
- Courage is the quality of mind that makes us forget how afraid we are.
- Courage is the brave foundation of all integrity.

DEFEAT & DETERMINATION

- The road to defeat is greased with the slime of indifference.
- Defeat is not bitter, if you don't swallow it.
- He who leaves home to set the world on fire often comes back for more matches.
- The only thing you get for nothing is failure.
- Most defeat comes from people that make excuses.
- Some men succeed because they are destined to, but most men succeed because they are determined to.
- He who doesn't climb the mountain cannot see the view.
- Curious people ask questions; determined people find answers.
- Our greatest glory is not in ever falling, but in rising every time we do.
- The secret of success is to start from scratch and keep on scratching.

- Better the shoulder to the wheel than the back to the wall.
- It's often the last key on the ring that opens the door.
- He who often starts many things finishes none.
- Perseverance is not a long race; it is many short races . . . one after another.
- Practice makes perfect.

DIRECTION & ENCOURAGEMENT

- The winds of God are always blowing, but you must set the sails.
- He who takes the wrong direction has a long road ahead.
- It isn't enough to make sure you're on the right track; you must also make sure you're going in the right direction.
- Success comes in cans; failure comes in cant's
- Correction can help, but encouragement can help far more.
- Appreciation is thanking, recognition is seeing, and encouragement is bringing hope for the future.
- Don't discourage another person's plans unless you have a better one to offer.

DIPLOMACY

- Being diplomatic is telling your boss he has an open mind, instead of telling him he has a hole in his head.
- Being diplomatic is patting someone on the head, instead of bashing it in.
- Smiling is the magic language of diplomacy.
- Diplomacy is cutting the other fellow's throat without using a knife.
- Diplomacy is the art of letting someone else have your way.
- Diplomacy is the art of turning a dropped stitch into a loophole.
- A true diplomat can put their best foot forward without stepping on anyone's toes.

DISCIPLINE

- Discipline is the refining fire by which talent becomes ability.
- The undisciplined man is a headache to himself and a heart-ache to others.
- The undisciplined are unprepared to face the stern realities of life.
- The cure for crime is not in the electric chair, but in the high chair.
- Discipline yourself so others won't need to.
- Discipline is embracing what we dislike as if we enjoy it.
- Discipline is the fuel that allows common people to obtain uncommon results.
- Persistence prevails when all else fails.
- Duty is what Right Reason demands and commands us to do.
- To bear what one thinks they cannot bear is truly to bear.
- Failure to try is self betrayal.
- It is one thing to consume a vice; another to be consumed by that vice.

- Self control is knowing that you can, but deciding that you won't.
- Be the master of your own mind, rather than be mastered by it.
- The ability to do something does not necessarily mean you must do it.
- Self awareness empowers us to examine our own thoughts.
- Be a function of your values rather than a function of your impulse.
- Self-mastery and self-discipline are the foundations of healthy relations with others.
- It is the weak that are cruel, for gentleness can only come from the strong.
- Accept responsibility for your own mistakes without seeking to find them in others.
- He who cannot change his thoughts cannot change his reality.
- Look to your own faults first.
- Discipline is the bridge between your goals and your accomplishments.
- Discomfort is a state of mind; discipline is a state of being.

DREAMS

- Some people who think they are dreamers are really just sleepers.
- It doesn't do any harm to dream, as long as you get up and hustle when the alarm goes off.
- It's more fun building castles in the air than on the ground.
- All air castles need a foundation.
- Castles in the air are all right until you start moving into them.
- You'll never make your dreams come true by oversleeping.
- Don't be too unhappy if your dreams never come true; just be grateful your nightmares don't.
- The poorest of all men is not the one without money, but the one without a dream.
- Our futures are created by what we dream today.
- We cannot dream ourselves into what we could be.

- Between tomorrow's dream and yesterday's regret is today's opportunity.
- No dream comes true until you wake up and get it done.
- A house is made of walls and beams; a home is built with love and dreams.

EDUCATION

- Learning can only become knowledge when it is assimilated in the mind of the student and shows in their character.
- Knowledge should not be pursued as an end in itself, but as a means towards the attainment of wisdom.
- Knowledge without experience is no knowledge at all.
- Knowledge should be subordinate to wisdom.
- Learning without thought is lost labor; thought without learning is perilous.
- Any mind can spot wrong answers, but it takes a creative mind to spot wrong questions.
- Once a mind is stretched to new ideas, it can never go back to its original dimension.
- Part of becoming wise, is knowing what to overlook.
- The structure of our thinking is the same as the structure of our language.

- As your vocabulary expands so will your thinking.
- Recognizing your ignorance is the first step towards wisdom.
- Teachers may open doors, but you must enter by yourself.
- Colors fade, temples crumble, and empires fall, but wisdom endures.
- Teaching is the most difficult of all the arts, and the most profound of all the sciences.
- People who don't read are no better off than people who can't read.
- Only the foolish continue with the same actions and expect different results.
- All wisdom must first begin with questioning.
- The first step towards wisdom is listening; the second step is listening.
- A moment of thought is worth more than an hour of talk.
- While you teach, you also learn.
- Not knowing is bad; not wanting to know is worse.
- Learning becomes amplified once it is shared.
- Curiosity is a characteristic of a vigorous intellect.

- Wise men read both books and life.
- Curiosity is nature's original school of education.
- Knowledge is secondary to imagination.
- The great aim of learning should be knowledge and action.
- Knowledge speaks but wisdom listens.
- Students may forget what we taught, but they will always remember how they were treated.
- Reading is to the mind, what exercise is to the body.
- Education alone, does not guarantee success.
- Education is no guarantee of intelligence.
- Everything you learn is useless, until put to use.

ENTHUSIASM & EXCELLENCE

- Enthusiasm is a good engine, but it needs intelligence for a driver.
- The gap between enthusiasm and indifference is filled with failures.
- Zeal without knowledge is fanaticism.
- Enthusiasm flourishes in adversity, kindles in the hour of danger, and awakens to deeds of renown.
- Enthusiasm can achieve in one day what reasoning must work at for centuries.
- Excellence is not a matter of chance but a matter of choice.
- Since every job is a self-portrait of the person who did it, autograph your work with excellence.
- A complete commitment is paramount to reaching the highest in performance.
- Some men dream of worthy accomplishments, while others stay awake and do them.

ENVY & FORGIVENESS

- People who cut you down are only trying to reduce you to their size.
- Only the jealous are quick to point out the negative, but rarely mention the positive.
- Only the envious attempt to undermine the reputation of others.
- Misery loves company.
- It is better to forgive and forget than to hate and remember.
- Only the kindest individuals can truly forgive and forget.

EXPERIENCE & FACTS

- Experience enables you to recognize a mistake when you make it again.
- Listen to the voice of experience.
- One thorn of experience is worth a whole wilderness of warning.
- Digging for facts is a much better mental exercise than jumping to conclusions.
- The hardest thing about facts is facing them.
- A sure way to end a red-hot argument is to lay down a few cold facts.
- Facts, when combined with ideas, constitute the greatest force in the world.

FLATTERY & SPEAKING

- Imitation is the sincerest form of flattery.
- Tell someone that they are too intelligent to be flattered, and flattered they are.
- Conscience is the only mirror that doesn't flatter.
- Criticism from a friend is better than flattery from an enemy.
- Often, it's not what we say, but how we say it.
- A good speech consists of a good beginning and a good end, preferably close together.
- Nothing is often a very good thing to say.
- The ability to speak several languages is valuable, but the art of keeping silent in one is precious.
- Swearing is the language of the ignorant.

FREEDOM & PATRIOTISM

- Freedom shall never come to those unwilling to fight for it.
- Evil will always flourish where it is unopposed.
- Good men must oppose tyranny in order to protect those who cannot protect themselves.
- Always question whether the ends justify the means.
- A true patriot must always question authority.
- Whoever would overthrow the liberty of a nation must begin by subduing the freedom of speech.
- The tree of liberty must be refreshed from time to time with the blood of patriots and tyrants.
- A benevolent despot still remains a despot.
- A civilized society is governed by its conscience.

- Freedom is not the right to do as you please, but the liberty to do as you ought.
- The protection of our rights can only endure with the performance of our responsibilities.
- Nothing dies so hard, or rallies so often, as intolerance.
- Democracies true test lies in respect for minority opinion.
- From the seeds of truth grow the trees of true liberty.
- A true patriot must always be willing to defend their country, even against its own government.
- It may begin by burning books, but often ends by burning men.
- A true patriot is always ready and willing to defend another's freedom of speech, even if they disagree with what's being said.
- Congress may pass bills, but taxpayers must pay them.
- A great society is measured by how it treats it's least fortunate.
- When a government commits mass deceit, being truthful may become treasonous.

FRIENDS & FAMILY

- The best way to keep your friends is not to give them away.
- Those who bring sunshine to the lives of others cannot keep it from themselves.
- Money can't buy friends, although it may buy a better class of enemies.
- Real friends will tell you of your faults and follies in prosperity, and assist you with their hand and heart in adversity.
- Every family tree produces some nuts.
- Children may tear up a house, but they never break up a home.
- It is easier to build boys than to mend men.
- True friendships have no betrayal.
- True friends are those who are there when needed.
- If a true friend cannot comfort you, they will share your discomfort.
- Never condemn others; rather see to it that you don't come short of your own mark.

- In the code of chivalrous honor, loyalty assumes paramount importance.
- Those who meet must one day part.
- What is hateful to you, do not do to others.
- Life without friendship is like the sky without the sun.
- If you want true friends, be a true friend.
- Telling the truth, means never having to remember what you said.
- The past is a mistress best shared.
- One loyal friend may be worth ten thousand relatives.
- A friend to all is a friend to none.
- A friend is a present you give to yourself.
- Only the great-hearted can be true friends; the cruel and cowardly can never know what true friendship means.
- Chance makes our parents but choice makes our friends.
- Envy is a mirror that reveals the bearers face more than anything else.
- There can be no friendship without confidence, and no confidence without integrity.
- By defending those who are absent, you retain the trust of those who are present.

- Consistency is the lifeblood of trust.
- The best way to remove your own problems is to help a friend solve theirs.
- Forget yourself for others, and others will forget you not.
- Being a good guest means knowing when to leave.
- The company you keep will determine the trouble you meet.
- To the world you may be only one person, but to one person you may be the world.
- A friend's eye can also be a good mirror.
- People may forget what you said but they will never forget how you made them feel.
- True friends can grow separately without growing apart.
- The secret to caring is to actually care.
- Good friends are like stars; you don't always see them, but you know they are always there.
- Disagreement is not disloyalty.
- Enemies may kill you, but only your loved ones can truly hurt you.
- True friends will side with you when you are in the wrong; anyone will side with you when you are in the right.
- Fences make for good neighbors.

- True friendships are a two way street.
- You are treated by others, based upon how you treat others.
- We may not remember the words of our enemies, but we will remember the silence of our friends.

GENEROSITY & HUMOR

- Give yourself to God, for He can do more with you than you can.
- What you are is God's gift to you, but what you make of yourself is your gift to God.
- The essence of generosity is self sacrifice.
- A rejected opportunity to give is also a lost opportunity to receive.
- Better to give an inexpensive gift with a smile, than an expensive one with a frown.
- No person was ever honored for what he received; always for what he has given.
- Humor is to life what shock absorbers are to vehicles.
- Humor is the lubricant of life's machinery.
- Our physical senses are incomplete without a sense of humor.
- If you can look into a mirror without laughter, you may not have a sense of humor.

GOALS & SUCCESS

- Choose a goal for which you are willing to exchange a piece of your life.
- Climb high and climb far; your aim is the sky and your goal is a star.
- A person who is going nowhere can be sure of reaching his destination.
- Creativity requires the courage to let go of certainties.
- Until you commit your goals to paper, you have intentions that are seeds without soil.
- It is no sin to attempt and fail; the only sin is not to make the attempt.
- Success depends upon individual initiative.
- You may be on the right track, but you'll get run over if you just sit there.
- Ideas are only as loud as the voices that carry them to the ears of the world.
- Ideas are only as effective as the hands that mold them into reality.

- Ideas are only as strong as the shoulders that bear them.
- If you're willing to live without everything, you can do anything.
- Anything worth doing is worth doing well.
- Today's preparation determines tomorrow's achievement.
- For success, attitude is as important as ability.
- Don't wait for opportunities, create them.
- Don't make excuses, make improvements.
- Winners will train, while losers complain.
- Never let your present situation dictate your future one.
- Many wish and dream, but few actually begin.
- If you never try, you'll never succeed.
- If you believe, you'll succeed; if you don't, you won't.
- Success favors the bold.
- The difference between ordinary and extraordinary is that little extra.
- Know your limits, and never stop trying to exceed them.
- A man can make great wealth, but great wealth does not make a man.

- You can dream, or you can do.
- You can be a talker, or a doer.
- If you are prepared to break your fall, you should be prepared for the fall itself.
- In failing to prepare, you prepare to fail.
- All hard work brings a profit, but mere talk leads to poverty.
- The secret of achievement is to not let what you're doing get to you, before you get to it.
- A man is rich according to what he is, not according to what he has.
- Falling down does not make you a failure; staying down does.
- The train of failure usually runs on the track of laziness.
- Don't mistake activity for achievement.
- One of the best ways to be successful is to follow the advice you give others.
- Ability may enable a man to reach the top, but character will determine if he stays there.
- It's not the number of hours you put in that counts, but rather how much you put into the hours.
- The poorest of all men is not the one without riches, but the one without dreams.

- The only preparation for tomorrow is the right use of today.
- The heart of a man cannot be determined by the size of his riches.
- Some succeed because they are destined to; most succeed because they are determined to.
- Some prizes lose their luster in changed circumstance.
- Either find a way, or make one.
- Every expert was once a novice.
- The best way to predict your future is to create it.
- Vision, without action, is only a dream.
- When you know better, you do better.
- Only those who risk going too far can determine how far they can go.
- Channel your positive thoughts towards positive gains.
- A bend in the road is not the end of the road.
- Your only limit is how high you can go.
- Substance is essential to achieving success.
- Success is never final; failure is never fatal. Only courage truly counts.
- Do not dwell on limitations, but focus on possibilities.

- The difference between a successful person and others is not a lack of strength or knowledge, but rather a lack of will.
- The only goal that can never be achieved is the one that is never attempted.
- He who looks outside only dreams; he who looks inside truly awakens.
- He who displays himself does not shine.
- Any who would climb a ladder, must begin at the first step.
- If you do what you have always done, you will get what you've always gotten.
- A goal is a dream with a plan and a deadline.
- The person who removes a mountain must first begin by carrying away small stones.
- Success is never final, and failure never total.
- One person practicing exceeds one thousand preaching.
- One cannot become what they need to be, by remaining what they are.
- The price of greatness must be responsibility.
- Success is measured by effort.
- True success is being able to spend your life in your own way.

- To accomplish great things, we must act as well as dream.
- It's not that some have willpower and others don't; it's that some are willing to change and others are not.
- Circumstance is temporary, but opportunity is perpetual.
- Excellence is not an act, but a habit.
- The only person it takes to change your life is yourself.
- If you aim for nowhere, that's where you'll go.
- Progress always involves risk.
- You can't steal second base, by keeping your feet on first.
- If at first you don't succeed, try and try again.
- Success often comes by taking a wrong step in the right direction.
- All the roads to success are uphill.
- Many people owe their success to advice they didn't take.
- The father of success is work; the mother of achievement is ambition.
- Abundance, unless used with the utmost care, destroys discipline.
- Great wealth and contentment seldom live together.

- Winners find ways to make things work; losers find excuses for why things don't work.
- Winners are those unafraid to take chances; losers wait around for the odds to improve.
- If you cannot win the race, make the one ahead of you break the record.
- Those who shoot at the sun, aim higher than those who shoot at a tree.
- While stopping too long to think, one often misses opportunity.
- History is written in books, but moments are written in the language of the heart.
- If you believe, you will succeed.
- Success breeds success.
- There is nothing wrong with climbing the ladder of success.

GOSSIP

- If you don't see it with your eyes, don't invent it with your mouth.
- Gossip is like winding up your tongue and then letting it go.
- When you plant a little gossip, you reap a harvest of regret.
- A tongue three inches long can ruin a man six feet tall.
- A dog is loved by old and young, for he wags his tail and not his tongue.
- Although the tongue weighs very little, few people are able to hold it.
- Ignorance is always swift to speak.
- He who throws dirt loses ground.

HAPPINESS & HEART

- Happiness is the inner joy that can be sought or caught, but never taught or bought.
- The surest way to happiness is to lose oneself in a cause greater than oneself.
- It's never too late to have a happy childhood.
- Worry doesn't help tomorrow's troubles, but it does ruin today's happiness.
- To handle yourself, use your head; to handle others, use your heart.
- People will judge you on your actions, not your intentions.
- In judging others, it's always wise to see with the heart as well as the eyes.
- Never worry about your heart till it stops beating.

HOME & HOPE

- A broken home is the world's greatest wreck.
- Home is where you hang your heart.
- Houses are built of brick and stone, but homes are made of love alone.
- Hope is the feeling that you will succeed tomorrow in what you failed at today.
- Hope is the first step to overcoming depression.
- He who has hope has everything.
- Hope is what makes us live today as if tomorrow were yesterday.
- Life without hope is life without meaning.

HONOR

- Those unwilling to fight for their honor have no honor.
- Better to die on your feet than live on your knees.
- Never bully the weak or turn your back on the strong.
- Perceiving what is right, and doing it not, is lack of courage.
- To run all kinds of hazards, and rush into the jaws of death for a righteous cause, is true valor.
- For a true warrior, when his stomach is empty it is a disgrace to feel hunger.
- A benevolent man is ever mindful of those who are suffering and in distress.
- There is no honor for the hunter to slay the animal which takes refuge in his presence.
- Intellect, itself, must be subordinate to ethical emotion.
- To know and to act should be one and the same.

- We should weep with those that weep, and rejoice with those who rejoice.
- Without sincerity, politeness is a farce and a show.
- Your word should be your bond.
- Honesty is always the best policy.
- A gentleman does not condemn lying as a sin, but as a weakness, and as such, highly dishonorable.
- Honor is a consciousness of personal dignity and worth.
- Dishonor is like a scar upon your soul, which grows larger as time passes by.
- Anger at a petty offense is unworthy of a superior man.
- It is within every man's mind to love honor; but little does he realize that what is truly honorable lies within himself and not elsewhere.
- The framework of honor is wisdom, benevolence, and courage.
- It's not the creed that saves the man, but the man that justifies the creed.
- Calmness of behavior and composure of mind should not be disturbed by passion of any kind.

- We must recognize in each virtue its own positive excellence and follow its positive ideal.
- When all honor is lost, it is a relief to die.
- It is indeed a poor soul who succumbs so easily to extraneous influences.
- Do not worry that you may be unknown, but rather seek to be worthy of being known.
- Everyone desires riches and honor, but if they can only be gained by committing evil, they must not be held.
- Accept the consequences of your own actions.
- Fear is the only thing you should actually fear.
- To have doubted one's own first principles, is the mark of a civilized man.
- No one makes a greater mistake than the person who did nothing, because they could only do a little.
- You cannot save honor with a lie.
- There is no right way to do what is wrong.
- Better to lose with honor than win through fraud.
- Better to be disliked for who you are, then liked for who you're not.

- If you feel it's something to hide, then you've crossed the line.
- Stand up for what is right, even if you're standing alone.
- What we are, communicates far more, than what we say.
- If you wish to be trusted, be trustworthy.
- Self-respect cannot be taken away if it is not given.
- A life of integrity is the most fundamental source of personal worth.
- The voice of conscience is so delicate that it's easy to stifle, but it's also so clear that it's impossible to mistake it.
- Excuses are a coward's sharpest weapons.
- Integrity is consistency between your values, goals, and actions.
- The only thing that evil needs in order to grow is for good people to do nothing.
- Better to die with a good name, than to live with a bad one.
- Be happy when your conscience hurts you, and very concerned when it doesn't.
- Reputation is made in a moment, but character is built in a lifetime.
- Take care of your character, and your reputation will take care of itself.

- To die for a worthy cause is the ultimate honor.
- Win with grace and lose with grace.
- Those with nothing to hide have nothing to fear.
- The naked truth is always better than the best dressed lie.
- Your vision will become clear, only when you look into your heart.
- Never overlook what is right for what is convenient.
- Extending your hand is extending yourself.
- No cost is too heavy for the preservation of your honor.
- Winning is not everything, but honor is.
- No task ahead of you is greater than the strength within you.
- Self-control is knowing you can, but deciding you won't.
- A strong man stands up for himself; a stronger man stands up for others.
- What is popular is not always right, and what is right is not always popular.
- Strong convictions precede great actions.

HUMILITY

- The person who does things that count doesn't usually stop to count them.
- One of the hardest secrets for a man to keep is his opinion of himself.
- To be humble to superiors is duty; to peers, courtesy; and to inferiors, nobility.
- Sincere humility attracts; lack of humility subtracts; and artificial humility detracts.
- Humility is remaining teachable.
- The most thankful people are the humblest.
- If you do not stay humble, you may stumble.
- The best way to be right or wrong is humbly.
- Those who look up to God rarely look down on others.
- Humility makes a man feel smaller as he becomes greater.
- The person who knows everything has a lot to learn.

INTEGRITY

- Always allow honesty and integrity to increase with your riches.
- Character is never erected on a neglected conscience.
- Character made by many acts may be lost by a single act.
- When you take care of your character, your reputation takes care of itself.
- Your youth and beauty may fade, but your integrity endures forever.
- Reputation is what you need to get a job; character is what you need to keep it.

KINDNESS

- Hatred and anger are often powerless when met by kindness.
- Kindness is the oil that takes the friction out of life.
- Kindness put off until tomorrow may become a bitter regret.
- Be kind to unkind people, for they need it the most.
- A kind word is better than a handout.
- Kindness pays most when you don't do it for pay.

LABOR & LAZINESS

- Success is sweet, but its secret is sweat.
- Some always arrive after the work is done.
- He who wishes to eat in the evening must be willing to work in the day.
- The trouble with a spouse who works like a horse during the day is that in the evening all they want to do is hit the hay.
- He who fiddles around seldom gets to lead the orchestra.
- It's difficult to soar with eagles when you associate with turkeys.
- Nothing is sadder than a student with a Mercedes mind but a Yugo performance.
- Poverty is often the partner of laziness.
- The surest way to crush whatever laurels you have won is to rest on them.
- Laziness is the mental alertness to avoid hard work.
- Disciplines inaction is indolence.

LAW

- No law has ever been passed that will keep a man from acting like a fool.
- Men fight for freedom and then start making laws to get rid of it.
- Ignorance of the law is what keeps our higher courts functioning.
- The arm of the law may sometimes need more muscle.
- Too many laws are passed ... then bypassed.

LEADERSHIP

- A leader knows where he is going, and is able to persuade others to follow.
- He who follows the leader won't be following the follower.
- He who stands at the head of the line must know where he's going.
- True leaders are ordinary people with extraordinary determination.
- Once a leader cultivates virtue, the people will flock to him.
- The best of leaders look upon an oath as derogatory to their honor.
- Real leaders can face all calamities and adversities with patience and a pure conscience.
- Worry not about not being in office, but rather worry about qualifying yourself for such a position.
- There is no need to preach when you show the way with your actions and your heart.

- Leaders are capable of seeing things in more than one way.
- Absolute power corrupts absolutely.
- With great power must come great responsibility.
- One earns respect by how they live, not by what they demand.
- Management is doing things right; leadership is doing the right things.
- Strong leaders build cultures that outlive them.
- An effective leader communicates with others that view things differently, and values those differences.
- Seek not to imitate the master, rather seek what they sought.
- Outstanding leaders have sources of inner direction.
- When you serve that which is corrupt, you become corrupt yourself.
- Put others before yourself, and you can become a leader among men.
- People don't care how much you know until they know how much you care.
- You can easily determine the caliber of a leader by the amount of opposition it takes to discourage him.

- The ability to hold a scalpel does not make one a surgeon.
- Leaders often blaze a trail for others to follow.
- Having power means assuming the obligation to use it responsibly.
- A true leader, must often set himself apart from those he leads.
- Leaders are individuals with the courage to go first.
- A man who has confidence in himself gains the confidence of others.
- One's rank does not confer privilege or power; it imposes responsibility.
- Leadership through anger will only get you so far.
- It is sometimes the burden of great leaders to make unspeakable choices.
- Leaders don't flock; you find them one at a time.
- A leader must sometimes sacrifice a finger, in order to save the hand.
- There can only be one chief for every tribe.
- A truly effective and confident leader carries his power; he's not carried by his power.

LIES & TRUTH

- A good memory is not needed if you always speak the truth.
- The truth is stubborn and doesn't apologize to anyone.
- Truth may not always be popular, but it's always right.
- The truth has only to exchange hands a few times to become fiction.
- Stretching the truth doesn't make it last any longer.
- Never be afraid to let the truth come to the top.

LIFE & DEATH

- Your past shapes you into who you are today.
- We are all judged by our actions.
- Attitude is a small thing that makes a huge difference.
- You will always miss all of the shots you never take.
- One cannot discover new oceans until you have the courage to lose sight of the shore.
- Do not follow the path; instead, blaze your own trail.
- Yesterday is but a dream; tomorrow a vision of hope; look to this day, for it is life.
- Although one cannot adjust the wind, they can adjust the sail.
- If it is to be, it is up to me.
- Never, ever, quit.
- Attitude is everything.

- Some make things happen; some watch things happen; some wonder what happened.
- He, who knows but one way, knows none.
- Chivalry is the poetry of life.
- Variety is the spice of life.
- Know thyself.
- To your own self, always be true.
- Trust in faith and destiny, but make things happen.
- A real man is unafraid to show his love.
- Think before you act.
- Modesty and respect for others feelings are the root of politeness.
- If there is something that needs to be done, there is certainly a best way to do it.
- Shame is the soil of virtue, morals, and good manners.
- Be forever mindful of your own short comings.
- When others blame you, blame them not; when others are angry at you, return not their anger.
- All human life has sorrow.
- All who are born must die.

- Do not do to others what you would not want others to do to you.
- Treat all life as you would like to be treated.
- All the negative energy you project into the universe will be projected by the universe back towards you.
- You must confront all that is painful, or you will be running away from yourself for the rest of your life.
- You cannot escape yourself.
- Enjoy where you are going more than where you've been.
- We are all trapped by what we've done.
- What's past is past.
- All men die, but not all men truly live.
- Strive for perfection, never for mediocracy.
- Life is what your thoughts make it.
- Life is not too short, it's just that many are dead for so long.
- Life is the art of drawing sufficient conclusions from insufficient premises.
- Words are whispers while actions are shouts.
- We cannot wash out the blood that stains our past, but we cannot allow it to destroy our future.

- Plan for the future in order to better process the present.
- When you hit rock bottom, there's really nowhere left to go but up . . . assuming you have the strength left to climb.
- Somewhere in the present lives a fragment of the past; somewhere in yesterday lies the key to the future.
- It's not what you mean to do that matters, but what actually gets done.
- Do not rush through life; pause and enjoy it.
- There are attempts and there are successes; history only remembers and praises one.
- Death is certain, while life is not.
- Think big thoughts, but relish small pleasures.
- Time is the true test of change.
- The heart and mind are capable of miraculous work.
- Whenever confronted by an opponent, conquer them with love.
- Be mindful of the future, but not at the expense of the present.
- If you're not pushing forward, you're sliding backwards.
- The greatest mystery of life is life itself.

- The past can never be changed, so strive for a better tomorrow.
- You can't change your past, but you can change your future.
- Make every decision count; you don't always get a second chance.
- One cannot step twice into the same river.
- Every exit is an entrance somewhere else.
- When making your choices in life, do not neglect living.
- One can't go back and make a brand new start, but you can start from new and make a brand new ending.
- You cannot be lonely if you like the person you're alone with.
- For everything you have missed, you have gained something else.
- Nothing last forever, not even your troubles.
- On your last breath, you will be more disappointed in the things you didn't do, rather than the ones you did.
- One never receives a second chance at making a first impression.
- Those who choose to live in denial may eventually be forced to live in fear.

- Heal your future by honoring your past.
- The bamboo that bends is stronger than the oak that resists.
- All are equal in death.
- What is does not need to be.
- True success cannot be achieved unless attained on both levels . . . inner and outer.
- All life has meaning.
- Perception governs how we see things; how we see things governs how we behave.
- Search your own heart with all diligence, for out of it flow the issues of life.
- We see the world not as it is, but how we are conditioned to see it.
- To achieve true happiness, you must generate positive energy and sidestep negative energy rather than empower it.
- Private victories precede public ones.
- Each of us guards a gate of change that can only be opened from the inside.
- You are what you are today because of the choices you made yesterday.
- True success is success with oneself.
- We are all free to choose our actions, but we are not free to choose their consequences.

- Not acknowledging a mistake, correcting it, and learning from it, is a mistake of greater magnitude.
- Be ashamed to die until you have won some small victory for mankind.
- You cannot talk your way out of problems you behaved yourself into.
- It is one thing to make a mistake, and another not to admit it.
- Dependency is a function of insecurity.
- Look beyond the obvious to discern the truth.
- One makes a living by what they receive; a life by what they give.
- The further backward you can look the further forward you can see.
- Peace of mind comes when your life is in harmony with true principles and values.
- There can be no death in the absence of life.
- That which we intend is not always what happens.
- Trust your feelings, but do not be ruled by them.
- Life is only a small part of what actually happens to us; and a huge portion of how we react to it.
- Your stand depends on where you sit.

- While the grass may look greener on the other side, it still needs to be mowed.
- Decisions may take you out of God's will, but never out of His reach.
- He who walks with wise men shall also be wise.
- Some complain about the thorns on roses, while others praise the roses among the thorns.
- The bridge you burn today may be the one you must later cross.
- The mighty oak was once a tiny seed that stood its ground.
- The measure of a man's character is not what he receives from his ancestors, but what he leaves to his descendants.
- Life can only be understood by looking backward, but it must be lived by looking forward.
- Always remember that time, not money, is irreplaceable.
- Those who bring sunshine to the lives of others cannot keep it from themselves.
- You can never win if you do not begin.
- Learn from the mistakes of others rather than making them yourself.
- When things go wrong, don't go wrong with them.

- The best way to get even is to forget.
- A man who is wrapped up in himself, makes a very small package.
- Kindness is the oil that takes the friction out of life.
- Better to die trying than to do nothing.
- The wisdom of the streets is paid for in pain.
- True confidence comes from acknowledging your own shortcomings.
- People are only as happy as they make up their minds to be.
- Worrying does not empty tomorrow of its troubles, but empties today of its strength.
- Change is a process, not an event.
- It is easier to live in blissful ignorance than in constant fear.
- External validation will never quiet the fires that rage within your soul.
- Madness and genius sometimes walk hand in hand.
- Your past is a rehearsal for the future.
- Never do the right thing the wrong way.
- Negative energy rebounds to pollute its source.
- The biggest step you'll make is the first one.

- Think twice and act once.
- Nourish the roses, but keep your eyes on the thorns.
- What you think you see is not always what transpires.
- One cannot over-consume without any regard to the effects of their ravaging.
- Lost time is never found.
- If you wish to be like someone else, you waste the person you are.
- Every choice you make defines who you are, what you are, and why you are.
- Do not judge the present without awareness to the past.
- The past cannot be changed; only the present and future lie within our hands.
- Life is a work in progress.
- He who stands on his toes does not stand firm.
- He who stretches his legs does not stand firm.
- He who stretches his legs does not walk easily.
- He who asserts only his own views is not distinguished.
- A man's life is his statement.
- Life is not without its share of wicked ironies.

- What begins must end.
- Those who accept death live in freedom and die in grace.
- Think, feel, and do.
- It is not the age that matters, but the substance.
- One cannot hide from the hidden.
- With resolution comes closure; with closure comes healing.
- When you learn from the past, you face the future with confidence.
- The best way to escape from a problem is to solve it.
- Life shrinks or expands in proportion to one's courage.
- A warm smile is the universal language of kindness.
- The greatest joy in life is to accomplish.
- All who would win joy must share.
- Patience, in one moment of anger, allows you to escape a hundred days of sorrow.
- A good instructor improves your skill; a great instructor improves your life.
- Have strength within and pride throughout.
- Possess your possessions; do not let them possess you.
- Self-reliance is the only road to true freedom.

- Suicide is a permanent solution to a temporary problem.
- If one allows others to continually take pieces of them, what will eventually be left?
- Behind every mystery awaits a truth to be told.
- Traveling the dark path inevitably leads to a dark end.
- We are what we repeatedly do.
- Without data or facts, all you have is an opinion.
- Talent is no guarantee of success.
- Admitting your own limitations is the first step in overcoming them.
- Dust is the final destiny of all great kingdoms.
- While life remains, hope endures.
- On the human chessboard, all moves are possible.
- You may be deceived if you trust too much, but you will live in torment if you do not trust enough.
- We are not put on this earth to see through one another, but to see one another through.
- Commitment, in the face of conflict, produces character.

- Only in giving ourselves to others, do we truly live.
- Discovery consists of looking at the same thing as others, but thinking something entirely different.
- It is better to fail in originality than to succeed by imitation.
- None are so blind, as those who will not see.
- You reap what you sow.
- Light comes to those who look for it.
- When you sow the wind, you reap the whirlwind.
- The youthful eye often lacks perspective.
- All living things must evolve or perish.
- Time may give, but it also takes away.
- Only fools and madmen live without fear.
- If you are to conquer tomorrow, you must first live today.
- No action goes without consequence.
- Action, to avoid grief, is a path to nowhere.
- You cannot win the future by hiding in the past.
- Others may doubt what you say, but they'll always believe what you do.
- Think twice, act once.

- You earn respect by how you live, not by what you demand.
- The biggest mistake is never learning from one.
- If you want things in your life to change, you have to change the things in your life.
- The only person who owes you anything is yourself.
- The value of health is usually realized after it's lost.
- If you want something you've never had, you must be willing to do what you've never done.
- If you want things to be different in your life, then you have to do things differently.
- Better to be happy and wealthy, than happy and poor.
- Life is what happens while you're making other plans.
- Live each day as if it were your last, for someday you'll be right.
- We make a living by what we get; a life by what we give.
- To begin a new life, you must first discard the old.

- If we forget our mistakes, we shall forever repeat them.
- Only when you are sin free, may you judge others.
- Watch your thoughts for they become your words; watch your words for they become your actions; watch your actions for they become your habits; watch your habits for they become your character; watch your character for it becomes your destiny.
- You can't get out of a hole by continuing to dig.
- The broader your tastes, the more versatile you are.
- Adulthood is not determined by age, career, education, or the ability to procreate; it is determined by maturity, responsibility, and self-sufficiency.
- Do not fear death; fear not living.
- Manhood is only reached when one becomes completely self-reliant.
- There can be no rainbows without rain.
- What doesn't move begins to rust.
- Comfort imprisons more people than prison bars.
- In order to maximize living, you need to maximize your interest.

- Most people are too busy earning a living, to have a life.
- You can either watch the lives of other people on television, or you can chose to live your own life.
- The last thing anyone will say on their deathbed is that they should have worked more overtime.
- Acknowledgement of one's own shortcomings is the first step in overcoming them.
- Where there's a will, there's a way.

LISTENING

- Some people only listen in order to gain time for a rebuttal.
- If a man wants his wife to listen, he should talk to another woman.
- Looking for a solution, without listening to the problem, is working in the dark.
- It takes great courage to stand up and speak; even greater courage to sit down and listen.
- Those that play by ear should remember that others also listen the same way.
- It's difficult to listen, while you're planning something you think needs to be said.
- One may have free speech, but that doesn't guarantee any listeners.
- The Creator still speaks to those who take time to listen.
- Your ears are not made to shut, but your mouth is.

LOVE

- Loving someone is seeing the best in them.
- Love without return is like a question without an answer.
- Never underestimate love at first sight; many of us would not pass a second inspection.
- Love is a fabric that never fades, no matter how often it is washed in the waters of adversity and grief.
- One of life's greatest learning is how to give and receive love.
- Love is seeking to make another person happy.
- Know your loyalties.
- A heart is never measured by how much you love; it is measured by how much you are loved by others.
- The bravest are often the most tender and the loving are often the most daring.

- Speak not of the materials which make the gift; speak of the spirit which prompts the gift.
- True loves do not seek to be part of each other's lives; they seek to be each other's lives.
- In love, man and woman become one flesh.
- True love is the merging of two minds and two souls in unison.
- Believe in your love, and you shall overcome all obstacles that fate may put in your path.
- The potential for tragedy haunts all who would dare to love.
- The way to love something is to realize it may be lost.
- A love that risks nothing is worth nothing.
- A relationship that does not end in peace does not end.
- Better to hurt with the truth, than mislead with a lie.
- One sting may be remembered longer than a thousand caresses.
- Life without love is not living.
- Hate can only carry you so far, before it turns inward and consumes you.

- True love can never be explained, only felt.
- Better to be occasionally cheated than perpetually suspicious.
- A pretty face is a dime a dozen; a heart of gold is a rare gem to be treasured.
- Only love can conquer hate.
- One may have all the riches in the world, yet without someone to share them with, they have nothing at all.
- True love is a single soul dwelling in two bodies.
- A true friend is one who is aware of all of your faults, and still accepts you.
- A love that can end, never really began.
- The heart that loves is always young.
- Love is like a fire; it can warm your heart or burn you down.
- An old man in love is like a flower in the winter.
- Brief is life, but true love is forever.
- True love is never without some jealousy.
- Love is the fire of life; it either consumes or purifies.
- The heart has its reasons, which reason knows nothing of.
- Old love rusts not.

- To be able to say how much you love is to love but a little.
- The only remedy for love is to love more.
- The pains of love are sweeter than all other pleasures.
- True love is two souls with a single thought and two hearts that beat as one.
- Age does not protect you from love, but love protects you from age.
- Absence makes the heart grow fonder.
- True love does not consist in gazing at each other, but in looking towards the same direction together.
- To live is to love.
- Never change once love has found its home.
- Love is the one part of us that is real.
- Love is the only service that power cannot command and money cannot buy.
- Nothing is impossible to a willing heart.
- To love and be loved is to feel the sun shine from both sides.
- The giving of love is an education in itself.
- Water cannot quench love, neither can floods drown it.
- A life without love is like a year without summer.

- The first duty of love is to listen.
- Absence sharpens love; presence strengthens it.
- True love is like ghosts; everyone talks about it but only a rare few have actually seen it.
- Love is the gift of oneself.
- Where there is great love, there are always miracles.
- Loving and being loved is life's only true happiness.
- To love is to receive a glimpse of heaven.
- Love demands all, and has a right to all.
- Love is immortality struggling within a mortal frame.
- He who finds not love finds nothing.
- The love we give away is the only love we keep.
- It is better not to live than not to love.
- Love is the key which unlocks all doors.
- Love is the only force capable of transforming an enemy into a friend.
- True love is one heart in two bodies.
- It is only the souls that do not love that go empty in this world.
- The most powerful force in the universe is love.

- Your true love will always understand what you do not say.
- Love is an act of endless forgiveness.
- When you truly want love, you will find it waiting for you.
- Falling in love is temporary; staying in love is forever.
- To love a person is to learn the song that is in their heart; and to sing it to them when they have forgotten.
- The tide of a man's heart may be turned by a woman's touch.
- If you wish to study love, study those who sacrifice for others.
- The measure of a man is not how great his faith is, but how great his love is.
- Your words are windows to your heart.
- Those who deserve love the least, deserve it the most.
- The heart is happiest when it beats for others.
- Hate can change, but love cannot.
- Hate is a choice, but love is a gift.
- No one is worth your tears, and the one who is won't make you cry.
- Love requires trust, and trust requires honesty.

- Love is a double edged sword; it can bring one to the heights of happiness or the depths of sadness.
- Too much time is wasted on searching for the perfect lover, instead of creating the perfect love.
- Regrets only come when you don't follow your heart.
- A relationship based on lies and deceit is doomed to fail.
- Money cannot buy true love or happiness.
- Without trust, there is no foundation for permanent success.
- Better to have loved and lost, than never to have loved at all.
- The true measure of a loving and caring heart is how much you are loved by others, not by how much you love.
- One may have to kiss many frogs before finding a prince or princess.

LOYALTY & MARRIAGE

- Loyalty often consists of keeping one's mouth shut.
- Loyalty is the root of all true friendships.
- Only a fool bites the hand that feeds him.
- A man without a wife is but half a man.
- He who marries for wealth sells his own liberty.
- Marriage has some thorns, but celibacy has no roses.
- Praise marriage not on the wedding day, but after many years.
- The most difficult years of marriage are those that follow the wedding.
- Love may intoxicate, but marriage sobers up.
- An ideal marriage is one where each party loves, cherishes, and encourages each other through all of the troubles caused by their marriage.
- Love may be blind, but marriage is an eye-opener.

- A successful marriage requires falling in love many times, always with the same person.
- A marriage may be made in heaven, but the maintenance must be done on Earth.
- Success in marriage is more than finding the right person; it's becoming the right person.

MISCELLANEOUS

- To leave the past where it belongs, one need only close the door on it.
- Poor planning on someone else's part does not constitute on emergency on your part.
- Justice carried to excess hardens into stiffness; benevolence indulged beyond measure sinks into weakness.
- He who has died in the bottom of his breast may no longer be harmed.
- For every action, there is an equal opposite reaction.
- All men hate what they fear most.
- Find a pattern and break it.
- Continually challenge yourself.
- Without educational credentials and/or experiential expertise, all one has is an opinion.
- Greed has no limits and envy has no boundaries, in the heart of a petty man.
- Even chaos has a pattern.

- The manner in which it was given is worth more than the gift.
- A stumble may prevent a fall.
- What matters most, must never be at the mercy of what matters least.
- If you're going to bow, bow low.
- Beneath the heaviest stone, lies the richest soil.
- Time is not measured by clocks, but by moments.
- See what others have seen, but think what no one else has thought.
- Never create what you can't control.
- Justice is blind, but not always just.
- A perfect murder not only eliminates the body, but the memory as well.
- Power has three components: those who want it, those who give it, and those who control it.
- Trust cannot exist in a vacuum.
- Suspicions are not proof.
- Justice is the constant desire and effort to render to every person their due.
- Play with heart; win with class; lose with dignity.
- Trust, like a human heart, can easily be broken.

- A madman is often nothing more than a broken genius.
- Fearful men make willing slaves.
- Ideals may be beyond our reach, but never beyond our fondest hopes.
- Keep your ideals high enough to inspire you, and low enough to encourage you.
- A poor man who marries a wealthy woman gets a ruler and not a wife.
- An American will cross the ocean to fight for democracy, but won't cross the street to vote in an election.
- Better to be judged by twelve, than carried by six.
- The needs of the many outweigh the needs of the few.
- Real men put the needs and wants of their family before their own.
- Manhood is determined by one thing alone . . . self-reliance.
- Differences challenge assumptions.
- There is no true greatness where there is not simplicity, goodness, and truth.
- Behind every mystery, waits a truth to be told.
- Just because you're from the ghetto, doesn't mean you have to be ghetto.

- A nation should not interfere in the affairs of another, until they have resolved their own issues.
- You can lead a horse to water, but you can't make it drink.
- A bird in the hand is worth two in the bush.
- Cream rises to the top.
- Two wrongs don't make a right.
- We provide the oxygen that feeds the media's flame.
- Desperate times call for desperate measures.
- Old habits die hard.
- Every cloud has a silver lining.
- To be truly beautiful, ones brains, personality, and inner qualities should outshine any and all outer beauty.
- Every rule has an exception; but the exception does not then become the rule.
- If you purchase an item you can't afford, then you don't own it . . . it owns you.
- Fiction usually makes sense, reality doesn't.
- When you're afraid to say what you want, you usually don't get what you want.

NEIGHBORS

- When your neighbor's house is on fire, your own property is in jeopardy.
- It is often easier to love humanity as a whole than to love your neighbor in particular.
- Nothing depreciates a car quicker than a neighbor buying a newer one.
- The ideal neighbor is the one who makes noise at the same time we do.
- One does not need to be an accomplished musician to play on their neighbors' nerves.

OPINIONS

- Some people fall for everything, and stand for nothing.
- Stand on your own two feet and you will grow in stature.
- Most of us appreciate a person who says what they think; especially if they think what we think.
- Opinionated people are like little rotund islands of complacency anchored in a sea of prejudices.
- Those who have great opinions of themselves are likely poor judges of human nature.
- Our strength is shown by what we stand for; our weakness by what we fall for.
- It is human to stand with the crowd; divine to stand alone.
- Knowledge is knowing the truth, and the truth cannot be captured by opinion alone.

- An opinion, formed by someone with an ego and false sense of their own worth, without the certified credentials to back it up are worthless.

PARENTING & CHILDREN

- Even the innocents have something to see.
- The tree will grow as the twig is bent.
- Parenthood is the art of bringing up children without putting them down.
- When parents don't mind what the children don't mind, then children don't.
- Treat a child as they are, and they will remain as they are; treat them as the person they can and should be, and they will become as they can and should be.
- A child's self image is created by the attitudes of those around them.
- The handling of children will bear fruit in the adults they are destined to become.
- As soon as independence has been reached, the parent who keeps on helping often becomes an obstacle.
- The most favorable time for a child to learn is when they wish to do so themselves.
- The role of adults is to respect what the child can do for themselves.

- When you tell a child they may forget; show them and perhaps they'll remember; involve them and they will understand.
- A man is never as tall as when he stoops to help a child.
- Small children give you headaches; big children, heartache.
- Children who are seen and not heard have just done something awful.
- The easiest children to bring up are calm and thoughtful, and belong to someone else.
- Children may be deductible, but they're still taxing.

PESSIMISM/OPTIMISM

- Pessimist, look at life through dark colored glasses.
- A pessimist thinks the sun sets in the morning.
- A pessimist is always good for bad news, never happy unless miserable, and burn their bridges before getting to them.
- Optimists see an opportunity in every calamity; pessimists see a calamity in every opportunity.
- The optimist is often as wrong as the pessimist, but is far happier.
- Optimism is a person's passport to a better tomorrow.
- No one has ever injured their eyesight by looking at the bright side of things.

PREPARATION

- Long range purposes keep you from being frustrated by short term failures.
- Those who do not know where they're going should not start their journey.
- Opportunity has the uncanny habit of favoring those who have paid the price of years of preparation.
- Prepare and prevent, instead of repair and repent.
- When you're thirsty, it's too late to think about digging a well.
- The price of mastery in any field is through preparation.
- It does not become someone else's responsibility to bail you out of a predicament you got yourself into.

PRIDE

- Temper is what gets most of us into trouble; pride is what keeps us there.
- Those who wrap themselves up in their own righteousness often complain of the cold.
- He who pats himself on the back may dislocate his shoulder.
- Always hold your head up, but keep your nose at friendly level.
- Do not let your pride become inflated, for you may have to swallow it someday.
- Nothing pleases a small man more than an opportunity to crack a big whip.
- Many a bee has been drowned in his own honey.

PROMISES & RESPONSIBILITY

- Promises are often made in storms and forgotten in calms.
- Promises are like money; easier made than kept.
- When you break your word, you break something that can't be mended.
- One thing that you can give and still keep is your word.
- Always keep your word.
- Many people blame failure on fate, but feel personally responsible for success.
- Some grow under responsibility, while others shrink.
- Privilege and responsibility are two sides of the same coin.
- He who buries his talent is making a grave mistake.
- Some people recognize their responsibilities in time to dodge them.

REPUTATION

- The circumstances amid which you live determine your reputation; the truth you believe determines your character.
- Reputation is what you're supposed to be; character is what you are.
- Reputation is the photograph; character is the face.
- Reputation comes over one from without; character grows up from within.
- Reputation is what one had when they come to a new community; character is what they have when they leave.
- Reputation is gained in an hour; character may take years.
- A single report gives you your reputation; a life of toil gives you your character.
- Reputation makes you rich or poor; character makes you happy or miserable.
- It's what you do when you have nothing to do, that reveals who you are.
- Reputation is what you need to get a job; character is what you need to keep it.

- White lies leave black marks on one's reputation.
- Every person has three names: the name they inherit, the name their parents give them, and the name they make for themselves.
- No one can build a reputation on what they plan for tomorrow.
- It is easier to acquire a good reputation than to lose a bad one.
- A slanderer only differs from an assassin in that he murders ones reputation instead of their body.
- Many men would turn over a new leaf if they could tear out some of the old pages.
- Everyone should fear death until they have something that will live on after their death.
- He who wants people to bet on him needs to have a good track record.
- People know what you are by what they see, not by what they hear.
- You cannot build a reputation on what you intend to do.
- If you can't shout it from the rooftops, you probably shouldn't be doing it.

- Everyone is the architect of their own character.
- Birds of a feather flock together.
- If you can't say something positive about others, then don't say anything at all.

SILENCE

- He who is a man of silence is a man of sense.
- Some people will not suffer in silence because that would take the pleasure out of it.
- Wisdom is made up of ten parts . . . nine of which are silence, and brevity is the tenth.
- One must speak up to be heard; but sometimes one needs to shut up in order to be appreciated.
- If there is a substitute for brains, it has to be silence.
- Talking comes by nature; silence by wisdom.
- Rest your chin in your hands when you think, for it will help keep your mouth shut so you won't disturb yourself.
- Discretion is putting two and two together, and keeping your mouth shut.
- Silence is the best way to hide ignorance.
- A man is known by the silence he keeps.

- People who can hold their tongues rarely have any trouble holding their friends.
- The hardest thing to keep is quiet.
- Wise men have open minds and closed mouths.
- If one keeps their mouth shut, they can't put their foot in it.
- Closed mouths catch no flies.

SINCERITY

- Sincerity is to practice more than your tongue says.
- A blush is one thing that can't be counterfeited.
- Sincerity is being yourself in any direction.
- Insincere praise is worse than no praise at all.
- Sincerity is the face of the soul.
- A hypocrite never intends to be what he pretends to be.
- Sincerity needs no witnesses.
- The sincere man suspects that he too, is guilty of the faults he sees in others.
- False doctrine is not right simply because a person sincerely believes it.
- Sincerity is the end and beginning of all things; without it there would be nothing.

SMILING

- The curve of a smile can set a lot of things straight.
- A warm smile thaws an icy stare.
- We all smile in the same language.
- A smile is God's cosmetic.
- Smiling is the lighting system of the face, and the heating system of the heart.
- When you see someone without a smile, give him one of yours.
- A smile is a wrinkle that shouldn't be removed.
- Smiling improves your face value.
- Smiling is the second best thing you can do with your lips.
- Wear a smile and have friends; wear a scowl and have wrinkles.
- The world always looks brighter from behind a smile.
- It takes seventeen muscles to smile, and forty-three to frown.
- Smiling confuses an approaching frown.

- If you didn't begin the day with a smile, it's not too late to practice for tomorrow.
- Smiling is a powerful weapon; you can even break ice with it.
- Smiling is a passport that takes you anywhere you want to go.

SPIRITUALITY

- Prayer is the key that opens God's mercies and blessings.
- It's a good idea to tune your instruments by prayer, before the concert of the day begins.
- Prayerfulness begets carefulness.
- Walk softly; speak tenderly; pray fervently.
- No God and no peace; know God and know peace.
- There will be no peace as long as God remains unseated at the conference table.
- Prayer must mean something to us, if it is to mean anything to God.
- Pray loudly enough to be heard by men, and sincere enough to be heard by God.
- Know from what failings your virtue springs.
- A mind is a living entity, and as such, is ever luminous.

- Our spirit and soul determine our being, not the crude matter that makes up our body.
- The spiritual aspect of valor is evidenced by calm presence of mind.
- Love, affection, and sympathy are the highest attributes of the human soul.
- One may reclaim their own soul by helping another reclaim theirs.
- The human body is but a shell to house the heart that beats within.
- Every soul, no matter how dark, carries some spark of light.
- If a body lacks a soul, only a statue can it be.
- Once you strip a man of his faith, all that's left is fear.
- To error is human, to forgive is divine.
- Without darkness, light cannot survive.
- Hate the sin, but love the sinner.
- Faith is believing, when all other senses tell you not to.
- All who live possess the keys to darkness.
- The eye with which you see God is the same eye with which God sees you.
- Forgiveness must first begin within your own heart.
- No one can hurt you, without your consent.

- It is more noble to give yourself completely to one individual, than to labor diligently for the salvation of the masses.
- We are not human beings having a spiritual experience; we are spiritual beings having a human experience.
- The mind retreats from what it cannot face.
- If you do not stand firm in your faith, you will not stand at all.
- If you don't want the fruits of sin, stay out of the devil's orchid.
- Faith is daring the soul to go beyond what the eyes can see.
- A clear conscience makes a soft pillow.
- If you seek, you will find.
- We all make mistakes, and have mistakes to forgive.
- Only when we come to terms with our own personal demons, may we achieve inner tranquility.
- The power that created you can also heal you.
- No matter how awesome the entity, it has a social contract with the rest of the universe.
- Good and evil are not always mutually exclusive.

- Only after destruction, can there be resurrection.
- Even darkness has its purpose.
- Only the spirit is true, not the façade of a label.
- The world is not given to us by our fathers; it is borrowed from our children.
- Do not look towards the stars, at the expense of looking within your own heart.
- The path to Eden is paved with swords and serpents.
- Forgiveness is an attribute of the strong.
- We cannot hope to scale great moral heights by ignoring petty obligations.
- Within every evil exists a more horrifying evil waiting to be released.
- Man is not God.
- Belief in God does not need to include belief in what man has said and/or written about God.
- The most dangerous quality to possess is misguided self-righteousness.
- The path to hell is paved with good intentions.
- Evil never sleeps.
- Only light can extinguish darkness.

- Evil flourishes when good people fail to act.
- The world at its worst needs the church at its best.
- One should always wish Merry Christmas to their Christian friends; Happy Hanukkah to their Jewish friends; and good luck to their atheist friends.
- Church membership does not make you a Christian any more than owning a piano makes you a musician.
- Do not mistake the words of the Church for the words of God.

TACT

- Tact is changing the subject without changing your mind.
- Someone who is tactful can keep their shirt on while getting something off of their chest.
- Tact is the art of taking sides without anyone knowing it.
- Being tactful is remembering a lady's birthday, but forgetting her age.
- Tact is knowing how far to go, before going too far.
- Social tact is making your guests feel at home, even though you wish they were.
- People with tact have less to retract.
- A wise man never tells a woman that she talks too much, but a tactful one tells her how beautiful she looks when her lips are closed.
- Tact is the ability to make a person see the lightning without letting him feel the bolt.

TEAMWORK

- It takes two to applaud.
- Cooperation is doing with a smile what you must do anyway.
- We may not always see eye to eye, but we should walk hand in hand.
- A bundle of sticks is always stronger than a single twig.
- Many people are lonely because they build walls instead of bridges.
- One should light the fire, while the other fans it.

TIME

- The lazier a man is, the more he plans to do tomorrow.
- Today is nature's way of giving yesterday another chance.
- Years do not come to be counted; they come to count.
- Never put off until tomorrow, what you can do today.
- Defer not until tomorrow to be wise, because for you tomorrow's sun may never rise.
- Yesterday is gone; forget it. Tomorrow never comes; forget it. Today is here; use it.
- Today is the blessed time of rest you could have enjoyed if only you did yesterday the things you were supposed to do the day before.
- All days are the same size, but some can pack more into them than others.

- One thing you can learn by watching the clock is that it passes the time by keeping its hands busy.
- Why is there never enough time to do it right, but always enough time to do it over?
- He who kills time injures eternity.
- If you must kill time, work it to death.
- No matter how hard you try to improve Mother Nature, you're not kidding Father Time.
- What Mother Nature gives, Father Time takes away.

TROUBLE

- When the shepherd speaks well of the wolf, the sheep are in trouble.
- When trouble moves in, make it pay rent.
- A lie is a coward's way of getting out of trouble.
- Kind words pick men up when trouble weighs them down.
- Nothing improves our prayer life faster than big troubles.
- Trouble is one product where the supply exceeds the demand.
- Troubles grow larger with nursing.
- He who talks without thinking runs more risk than he who thinks without talking.

TRUST

- A man who trusts God is a man who can be trusted.
- Once trust is broken it may be repaired, but it is never quite the same.
- He who cannot mind his own business should not be trusted with the business of others.
- He who trusts his own heart is a fool.
- Trust God for the unexpected, and let him surprise you by doing the unexplainable.

UNDERSTANDING

- Make sure you reject only ideas, and not the people behind them.
- Never judge another, until you have walked in his footsteps.
- Instead of putting others in their place, try putting yourself in their place.
- People who truly understand each other never fight.
- A clever man tells a woman he understands her; a stupid one tries to prove it.
- The best way to be understood is to be understanding.

WISDOM

- Wisdom is common sense taken to an uncommon degree.
- Wisdom is knowing less, but understanding more.
- Fools say, "I can't"; the wise say, "I'll try."
- A fool tells what he will do; a wise man does it and says nothing.
- A great deal of trouble has been caused by too much intelligence and too little wisdom.
- As one becomes wiser, they talk less and say more.
- Wise words are sometimes spoken in jest, but many more foolish ones are spoken in earnest.
- No one is right, all of the time.
- Those who recognize their faults, have the best chance to correct them.

WORDS

- Keep your words soft and sweet, for one day you may have to eat them.
- Sharp words make more wounds than doctors can heal.
- Expenditure of words beyond the income of ideas is wasteful.
- A spoonful of honey will catch more flies than a gallon of vinegar.
- Tart words make no friends.
- Words should be weighed, not counted.
- Do not stop to pick up the kind words you've dropped.

YOUTH

- In order to stay youthful, stay useful.
- The greatest danger that confronts the younger generation is the example set by the older one.
- Youth and beauty fade, but character endures forever.
- You are young only once, so if you act foolish after that, you'll have to find some other excuse.
- Age is the best fire extinguisher for flaming youth.
- You are young at any age, if you are planning for tomorrow.
- It is one thing to be young and dumb; another to be old and still dumb.
- Youth is not an age, but a state of mind.
- You are as young as your faith, as old as your doubt, as young as your self-confidence, as old as your fear, as young as your hope, and as old as your despair.